Irish Traditional Melodies

Volume 1

Jigs

Reels

Polkas

Hornpipes

And More

Compiled and arranged

by

Frank Edgley

Irish Traditional Melodies, Volume 1
by Frank Edgley

ISBN-13: 978-1-953208-34-7

Also by Frank Edgley:

Irish Traditional Melodies, Volume 2 (Rollston Press, 2026)

The Anglo Concertina Handbook of Tunes and Methods for Irish Traditional Music (Rollston Press 2023)

ROLLSTON PRESS
1717 Ala Wai Blvd #1703
Honolulu, HI 96815
USA
www.rollstonpress.com

Contents

Reels

Jigs

Slip Jigs

Slides

Hornpipes

Polkas

Miscellaneous

Forward

These tunes are the result of years of teaching and playing Irish music on the concertina. They reflect my own musical tastes, for the most part, and are tunes which are either common session tunes, or tunes which I believe should be introduced to musicians so that, one day, they may find their way into session repertoires. The arrangements are mine. At least they are the way I play them, more or less. They have been purposely left in a fairly simple form so that each musician, whatever his or her ability, may play them. I have written most of them out in full, so that this book can be used as a sort of notebook, and changes or variations can be made more easily without affecting other parts of the tune. For example, changes can be made in the second eight bars which would be difficult to notate if written out with repeats. Most of the "composers" of these tunes are unknown to me, and many of these tunes have reached their "final" state through a process of metamorphosis. Phrases of one tune find their way into another tune and so many of these tunes are the result of an unconscious collaboration of generations of musicians. To those musicians who should be associated with any of the tunes in this book and are not recognized, I apologise. Many thanks to my friend, Chris Droney, of Bell Harbour, County Clare for permission to use his tunes.

Statement of Purpose

This book is intended for the educational purposes of teaching and disseminating traditional Irish music. If you are aware of any tunes which appear in this book to which credit has not been given, please contact me so that this error may be corrected.

At FEdgley@cogeco.ca

Also Available from Frank Edgley:

"Bridges" (CD of traditional music, on concertina)

"The Anglo Concertina,, a Handbook of Tunes and Methods"-concertina tutor

The Edgley Concertina-handcrafted anglo concertinas

Ah, Surely!

reel

The Blackberry Blossom

single reel

The Bell Harbour Reel

Chris Droney

The Broken Pledge

reel

Chris Droney's Reel

Chris Droney

Come West Along the Road

reel

The Connemara Stocking

reel

Grandpa Tommy's Ceili Band

reel

The Dublin Reel

single reel

Father Kelly's

reel

The Foxhunters

reel

The Galway Rambler

single reel

The First House in Connaught

reel

Hold the Reins

single reel

Miss Thornton's

Reel

Miss Monaghan

reel

Mrs. McLeod's

reel

trad. arr.by F. Edgley

The Old Bush

reel

The Peeler's Jacket

single reel

The Redhaired Lass

single reel

20

The Sally Gardens

reel

The Shannon Breeze

(Rolling in the Ryegrass)

single reel

The Silver Spear

reel

The Swallow Tail Reel

reel

arr. by Frank Edgley

Austin Barrett's

double jig

Banish Misfortune

double jig

The Blackthorn Stick

jig

The Cook in the Kitchen

double jig

Fasten the Leg on Her

double jig

Gallagher's Frolics

jig

The Geese in the Bog

double jig

Gillian's Apples

double jig

Have A Drink With Me

double jig

Hogan's

double jig

traditional
arr. F.Edgley

The Humours of Ennistymon

double jig

The Idle Road

double jig

The Kesh Jig

The Lark in the Morning

double jig

The Legacy

double jig

The Mug of Brown Ale

(The Winter Apples --- Jig)

Trad. Arr. by F. Edgley

Old Man Dillon

double jig

Palm Sunday

double jig

Petticoat Loose

double jig

The Pretty Girl

Jig

Saddle the Pony

double jig

Sean Bui

(Yellow John)

Tatter Jack Walsh

double jig

The Tongs by the Fire
double jig

When the Cock Crows It is Day

double jig

Unknown

double jig

Barney Brallaghan

slip jig

The Boys of Ballisodare

slip jig

The Bank of Turf

slide

The Brosna Slide

slide

The Old Favourite

slide

The Scartaglen Slide

slide

The Weaver's Slide

slide

Colin Edgley

hornpipe

Frank Edgley

contact FEdgley@cogeco.ca

Cronin's

hornpipe

The Cuckoo

hornpipe

1.
2.

The Poor Old Woman

hornpipe

The Rover through the Bog

hornpipe

The Stack of Wheat

hornpipe

The Wicklow Hornpipe

hornpipe

Along the River Bank

polka

The Ballydesmond Polka

polka

Dan Callaghan's

Polka

Egan's

polka

The Gneevgullia Polka

polka

Jerome Burke's

polka

John Walsh's

polka

Lackagh Cross

polka

trad. arr by F. Edgley

The Little Diamond

polka

The Maid of Ardagh

polka

Maurice Manley

polka

Peggy Ryan's

polka

Red Haired Mary

polka

Sweeney's

polka

The Tournmore Polka

polka

The Tourniore Lasses

polka

trad. arr. by F. Edgley

The Unknown Polka

polka

The Cumann na Bhan are Dead and Gone

quadrille

The Donegal Mazurka

mazurka

Fanny Power

planxty

Maggie Brown

set dance

Mrs.Ellen O'Dwyer's Fancy

barn dance

Planxty Irwin

planxty

Turlough O'Carolyn

Rodney's Glory

set dance

She Hasn't the Knack

quadrille

Si Bheg Si Mhor

planxty

Sleive Aughty

March

The South Wind

air

The Sweet Maid of Glendaurel

barn dance

Irish Traditional Melodies V.1

Reels

Jigs

(Jigs continued on Vol.2)

Irish Traditional Melodies Volume 2

Jigs (cont.)

Slip Jigs

Slides

Hornpipes

Polkas

Miscellaneous

The Graduate

REEL

For Gwen Edgley's Graduation - University of Windsor

Composer Frank C. Edgley
Dec.14, 2005

The Blue-eyed Rascal

set dance

Colin Edgley

hornpipe

Frank Edgley

contact FEdgley@cogeco.ca

For Those Who Went Before

air

Rubato

Frank C. Edgley

6

10

14

1.

18

2.

22

Expr

26

Kathleen Davison-Remel

About the Author

Frank Edgley has been involved as a performer and teacher of "Celtic" music for over 40 years. In the 1970's, under his direction, The Scottish Society of Windsor Pipe Band won the North American, Inter-Provincial, Canadian, and U.S. Pipe Band Championships two years in a row.

In the early 1980's, he became interested in Irish traditional music, and began to play, among other things, the Anglo concertina. He has performed at various festivals in Ontario and Michigan, including the following festivals: Saline, Celtic Spirit, AACTMAD (Ann Arbor), Windsor, and Goderich, Ontario. In Ireland, he as performed at the Mrs. Crotty Concetina Festival, at the concertina concert at the "Willie Clancy Week", at Milltown Malbay, and has compete at the All-Ireland Fleadh.

For five years, Frank has been one of the staff teachers at the Celtic College in Goderich and has also taught concertina at the Milwaukee Celtic Summer School. He is one of North America's most recognized concertina repairmen, and builds fine hand-crafted Anglo concertinas commercially. He and his son, Frank J. Edgley, have produced a CD, titled *Bridges*, featuring the concertina and other traditional instruments.

www.ingramcontent.com/pod-product-compliance
Lightning Source LLC
LaVergne TN
LVHW080324110826
845155LV00026B/187

* 9 7 8 1 9 5 3 2 0 8 3 4 7 *